THE OUTDOORS

DEEP-SEA FISHING

by Tyler Omoth

FOCUS READERS

WWW.FOCUSREADERS.COM

Focus Readers is distributed by North Star Editions:
sales@northstareditions.com | 888-417-0195

Produced for Focus Readers by Red Line Editorial.

Photographs ©: Neophuket /iStockphoto, cover, 1; Scott Leigh/iStockphoto, 4–5; Jodi Jacobson/iStockphoto, 6; grandriver/iStockphoto, 8–9; holbox/Shutterstock Images, 10, 22–23; Neophuket/Shutterstock Images, 13; Ivan Sabo/Shutterstock Images, 14 (top left); carebott/iStockphoto, 14 (top right); dlewis33/iStockphoto, 14 (bottom left); temmuzcan/iStockphoto, 14 (bottom right), 16–17; dobok/iStockphoto, 15 (top left); Peter Spiro/iStockphoto, 15 (top right); Arena Creative/Shutterstock Images, 15 (bottom left); Homiel/iStockphoto, 15 (bottom right); Przemyslaw Wasilewski/Shutterstock Images, 19; Cecop aLp/Shutterstock Images, 20; EML/Shutterstock Images, 25; Igor Zaytsev/Shutterstock Images, 26–27; AirLandSea/iStockphoto, 29

ISBN
978-1-63517-226-3 (hardcover)
978-1-63517-291-1 (paperback)
978-1-63517-421-2 (ebook pdf)
978-1-63517-356-7 (hosted ebook)

Library of Congress Control Number: 2017935873

Printed in the United States of America
Mankato, MN
June, 2017

ABOUT THE AUTHOR

Tyler Omoth is the author of more than two dozen books for children on topics ranging from baseball to Stonehenge to turkey hunting. He loves going to sporting events and taking in the sun at the beach. Omoth lives in sunny Brandon, Florida, with his wife.

TABLE OF CONTENTS

THE THRILL OF THE CATCH

It's a perfect day on the water. You are riding on a fishing boat on the Pacific Ocean. Three heavy-duty fishing poles stretch as their lines drag in the water.

Suddenly, one pole lurches. The reel whines as it spins out line. There's a fish on the other end, and it's big.

A fishing boat sails near Santa Catalina Island in California.

The mahi-mahi, sometimes called the dorado, is known for its bright colors.

The fish pulls hard on your line as the captain straps you into the harness. You fight to reel in the fish for nearly an hour. Finally, you get it inside the boat. There will be delicious **mahi-mahi** on the table tonight.

People have gone deep-sea fishing for thousands of years. At first they used hooks made of bone to catch fish. They sailed crude rafts. As people created better tools and boats, they could fish in deeper waters. Motorized boats allowed people to travel quickly. It became easier to reach good fishing spots.

Today, people can hire **charter boats** to take them out onto the water. They may also use **GPS** navigation to find their way around the oceans.

FISHING DESTINATIONS

People travel all over the world in search of the biggest fish. Nova Scotia is known for prize tuna. Giant blue marlins can be found in Australia, and Costa Rica is famous for record-size mahi-mahis.

OUT ON THE WATER

Deep-sea fishing is sometimes called offshore fishing. This kind of fishing is done in water that is at least 100 feet (30 m) deep. Deep-sea fishing boats sail out to the deeper waters of oceans and gulfs. The boats must be strong enough to handle strong waves and currents.

Deep-sea fishing boats often have fishing rod holders.

Some anglers use special chairs for support as they reel in huge fish.

Deep-sea **anglers** catch big fish that cannot be found near shore. They use heavy-duty fishing rods. These rods are strong enough to withstand the fish's pulling. But they are also flexible.

A reel at the base of the rod holds the fishing line. Deep-sea fishing line is strong and flexible. A float or bobber is attached to the line. It helps the line float in the water. This sets the depth of the bait or **lure**.

When an angler catches a fish, he or she must remove the hook from the fish's mouth. Many anglers use a needle-nose pliers. This tool has a long, pointed nose. It keeps the angler's fingers safe while handling the sharp hook.

Many species of fish have weight limits. Anglers can only keep fish that are over a certain weight. A lip-grip scale allows anglers to weigh their catch right away.

This scale can be hooked onto the fish's mouth. Some fish species may also have length requirements. For this reason, many anglers carry a tape measure. They use it to tell if a fish is the right size.

If the fish is big enough to keep, it can be prepared for storage. Many anglers use a long, thin knife called a fillet knife. They cut the fish's meat into narrow strips.

Sport fishermen are people who go fishing just for fun. They do not eat the fish they catch. Instead, their goal is to enjoy the thrill of hooking a huge fish. Sport fishermen often fish for sailfish and blue marlins. They may even try to catch sharks.

A wahoo's impressive size and speed make it an exciting catch for deep-sea anglers.

Other anglers prefer to catch fish that are good for eating. These fish are often smaller, but they are still powerful enough to provide a thrilling catch. Many people catch and eat mahi-mahis. Wahoos and groupers are also common targets.

DEEP-SEA FISHING SUPPLIES

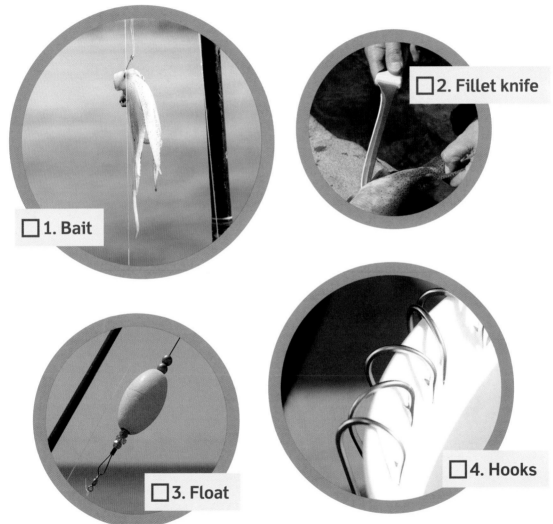

☐ 1. Bait

☐ 2. Fillet knife

☐ 3. Float

☐ 4. Hooks

☐ **5. Lip-grip scale**

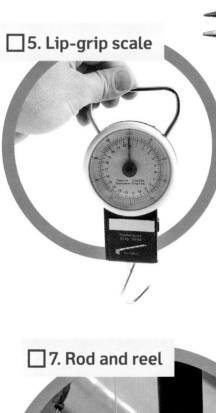

☐ **6. Needle-nose pliers**

☐ **7. Rod and reel**

☐ **8. Tape measure**

HOW TO FIND FISH

Before fishing, anglers study the kind of fish they hope to catch. This helps them choose the best bait to use. Anglers also look for places where fish tend to feed. Offshore structures such as **reefs** and canyons are good fishing spots. Even sunken ships can provide a good place for fish to eat.

Many deep-sea anglers use mackerel as bait.

One of the best ways to find fish is to watch for signs above the water. When groups of birds gather on the open water, it usually means there are bait fish nearby. Areas with bait fish often have larger fish as well.

Modern equipment such as fish-finding devices can also help find good locations. These devices use **sonar** to show when schools of fish pass below the boat.

There are three basic methods for deep-sea fishing. Anglers choose a method based on what type of fish they want to catch. They may also pick the best method for the area where they are fishing.

A group of birds flies over the water as an angler fishes for cod.

In one method, anglers let the bait and line drag in the water behind the boat. This method is known as trolling. It is a good way to catch fast, aggressive fish.

Trolling is a good way to catch sailfish, wahoos, and tuna.

Trolling anglers often keep several lines in the water at one time.

Bottom fishing is another common method. In this method, anglers use a sinker to weigh the line down. The sinker sits on the ocean floor while the bait and hook float nearby. Bottom fishing is a good way to catch fish that feed along the ocean floor.

The third deep-sea fishing method is called casting. Anglers use their fishing rods to throw the bait out on the water. Then they reel the line back toward the boat. The boat moves very slowly when an angler is casting. Sometimes it does not move at all.

Casting works well for fish that hide under structures such as rocks and reefs. Snappers and amberjacks are often caught using this method.

SAFETY TIPS

Every fishing boat should carry safety gear. There should be one life jacket for each person on board. Children should always wear their life jackets.

Flares can be used to signal other boats in case of an emergency. Every boat should also carry an emergency position-indicating radio beacon (EPIRB).

Wearing a life jacket is an important part of water safety.

This device sends out a signal. It can tell rescue teams where to find the boat.

Before leaving for a deep-sea fishing trip, anglers should create a float plan. This plan tells where the boat will be going and what time it is expected to return. Anglers should share this plan with someone who is not going on the trip. That way, someone on shore always knows where the boat will be.

Fishing during storms and windy weather is dangerous. It is important for anglers to pay attention to weather forecasts. Boats should have a radio on board. This allows anglers to monitor the forecast as the day goes on.

EPIRBs help rescue teams respond quickly or even find a boat's exact location.

The fish themselves can be dangerous, too. Some kinds of fish have sharp teeth. Others have poisonous stingers. Anglers should research the fish they hope to catch. They should study other common fish in the area, too. Learning the proper way to handle each kind of fish can help prevent injuries.

CONSERVATION

All deep-sea anglers must purchase a fishing license. Money raised from the sale of fishing licenses is used to protect the fish's **habitats**. Anglers can help protect these habitats, too. They should avoid dumping litter or liquids into the water. Instead, they should throw away trash after they get back to shore.

Anglers can help protect fish and their habitats.

Anglers also need to know the size and quantity guidelines for the fish they catch. They should not keep fish that are too small. Releasing small fish helps more fish survive to become adults.

It is also important to handle fish as carefully as possible. Anglers must be gentle when removing hooks. They should

CIRCLE HOOKS

Most hooks are J-shaped. But circle hooks are less likely to harm fish. Circle hooks are more likely to hook a fish in the lip or jaw than J-shaped hooks. If a fish swallows a circle hook, it will not hook the fish's stomach. Instead, the hook will slide back out to the mouth. This protects the fish's organs.

An angler removes the hook from a marlin's mouth.

also be careful not to keep too many fish. By releasing any fish they do not intend to eat, anglers help make sure there will be plenty of fish in the future.

FOCUS ON
DEEP-SEA FISHING

Write your answers on a separate piece of paper.

1. Write a paragraph describing the main ideas of Chapter 2.

2. Do you think conservation rules are too strict? Why or why not?

3. What do anglers use to weigh the fishing line down?
   - **A.** a bobber
   - **B.** a sinker
   - **C.** a lure

4. Why would trolling not be a good method for catching bottom-feeding fish?
   - **A.** Trolling does not use hooks.
   - **B.** Trolling will not move the bait quickly enough.
   - **C.** Trolling keeps the bait too high up in the water.

Answer key on page 32.

GLOSSARY

anglers
People who fish with a rod, reel, and line.

charter boats
Boats that can be reserved for private trips.

GPS
A navigation system that uses satellites to figure out location.

habitats
The type of places where plants or animals normally grow or live.

lure
An artificial bait used to attract and catch fish.

mahi-mahi
A large fish with a long fin along its back that is often caught by deep-sea anglers.

reefs
Ridges of sharp rock, coral, or sand just below the ocean surface.

sonar
A system for measuring distances and finding objects underwater by sending sound pulses.

TO LEARN MORE

BOOKS

Carpenter, Tom. *Saltwater Fishing: Snapper, Mackerel, Bluefish, Tuna, and More*. Minneapolis: Lerner Publications, 2013.

Hamilton, S. L. *Big Game Fishing*. Minneapolis: Abdo Publishing, 2015.

Pendergast, George. *Deep-Sea Fishing*. New York: Gareth Stevens Publishing, 2015.

NOTE TO EDUCATORS

Visit **www.focusreaders.com** to find lesson plans, activities, links, and other resources related to this title.

INDEX

Answer Key: **1.** Answers will vary; **2.** Answers will vary; **3.** B; **4.** C